AR PTS
2.0
AR RL
7.40

W9-BAK-377

DATE DUE

			Printed in USA

WOMEN OF SPORTS

THE BEST OF THE BEST

in Tennis

BY
RACHEL RUTLEDGE

M
THE MILLBROOK PRESS
BROOKFIELD, CONNECTICUT

Produced by
CRONOPIO PUBLISHING
John Sammis, President
and
TEAM STEWART, INC.

Series Design and Electronic Page Makeup by
JAFFE ENTERPRISES
Ron Jaffe

Researched and Edited by
Mark Stewart and Michael Kennedy

All photos courtesy
AP/ Wide World Photos, Inc.
except the following:

RICH KANE/SPORTS CHROME
Cover photo (Martina Hingis at the 1997 U.S. Open)

TEAM STEWART, INC.
Page 6

Printed in the United States of America

Published by
The Millbrook Press, Inc.
2 Old New Milford Road
Brookfield, Connecticut   06804

Library of Congress Cataloging-in-Publication Data

Rutledge, Rachel.
 The best of the best in tennis / by Rachel Rutledge.
 p.   cm.   —(Women of Sports)
 Includes index.
 Summary: Discusses the past and future of women's tennis and presents biographies of eight
of the sport's most famous players: Lindsay Davenport, Steffi Graf, Martina Hingis, Anna
Kournikova, Mary Pierce, Aranxta Sanchez Vicario, Monica Seles, and Venus Williams.
 ISBN 0-7613-1303-6 (lib. bdg.).—ISBN 0-7613-0445-2 (pbk.)
 1. Women tennis players—Biography—Juvenile literature. 2. Tennis—Juvenile literature.
[1. Tennis players. 2. Women—Biography. 3. Tennis] I. Title.   II. Series.
GV994.A1R88 1998
796.342'092—dc2l
[B]   98-25260
                                                                                          CIP
                                                                                           AC

pbk: 10 9 8 7 6 5 4 3 2 1
lib: 10 9 8 7 6 5 4 3 2 1

CONTENTS

In the
Beginning

The history of tennis dates to the ball-and-paddle games played since medieval times, and perhaps even farther back than that. There is clear evidence that the ancient Romans played games remarkably similar to tennis. "Modern" tennis began about 125 years ago, when Walter Clopton Wingfield, a retired British Army major, introduced a game he called "Sphairistike" to some of his wealthy friends at a pheasant shoot in Wales. Wingfield believed there was a need for an outdoor game men and women could enjoy together, and it turned out he was right. "Lawn tennis," as it came to be called, was a huge and immediate success among members of the upper class. Only four years after the major's introduction, the first tournament was played at the All-England Croquet and Lawn Tennis Club in the town of Wimbledon.

The role of women at that historic event was limited to clapping politely after points, but that is not to say that tennis lacked an enthusiastic following among females. On the contrary, women were playing the sport and enjoying it immensely in every corner of the British Empire. In 1884, the first major tennis tournament for women was held at

Wimbledon. The winner's prize was a silver hair brush. In 1887, the first women's tournament in the U.S. was played in Philadelphia. Tennis at this time was not the fast, hard-hitting game it is today. In fact, women generally competed in heavy, cumbersome skirts which came down around their ankles. Overhand serving was unheard of, and the most aggressive offensive tactic was the chop stroke, which deadened the ball when it hit the grass.

Things began to change during the 1890s, when a British woman named Lottie Dodd raised eyebrows at Wimbledon with her powerful strokes from the baseline and her deft volleying. Over the next two decades, the women's game got faster and more competitive, thanks in part to an influx of players from California, where the game owed less to the genteel conventions of the East Coast country club set. The first truly dominant player was Molla Bjurstedt, the seven-time Scandinavian champion, who took up residence in the U.S. in 1915. She won by mounting an unrelenting attack on opponents, hitting every shot as hard as she could and finishing points with crackling winners or powerful overhead volleys. It took other players nearly a decade to catch up to her.

During this time, one of the top players in the world was Eleanora Sears. The product of a well-known and respected New England family, she was America's first female multisport athletic star. Besides her tennis championships, Eleanora was an excellent swimmer, golfer and squash player, and she could handle a rifle as well as any man. She flew airplanes, skippered yachts and raced powerboats. In the years before World War I, a great debate was raging in the U.S. about the value of women's sports. A majority of Americans believed that exercise was physically harmful to the female body, and that sports robbed young ladies of their feminine attributes. A growing number of women, however, believed that only good things could come from exercise and competition. Sears used the publicity she received as a tennis star to promote the value of women's athletics to a nationwide audience.

Suzanne Lenglen brought an intriguing combination of glamour and guile to the court. She also was the first woman who figured out how to make tennis pay.

After the First World War, a flamboyant young Frenchwoman named Suzanne Lenglen was doing things on the court no one had ever seen before. Hers was not a power game, but a game of esthetic beauty and dramatic flourishes. Lenglen moved like a ballerina, yet she also had a head for tennis—she could dictate play to her liking and rarely missed an opportunity to put a ball away. What spectators found so enchanting, though, was that she did not subscribe to the game's stodgy "uniform." Instead, the French star wore light, flowing dresses that revealed her knees during play, and sported brightly colored headbands or stylish hats. She ruled women's tennis in England and France, and was rightly considered a national treasure. During the winters, her matches on the French Riviera attracted thousands of spectators.

In the 1920s, women's tennis began to generate income for promoters for the first time. Like all tennis players back then, Suzanne Lenglen was an amateur. She received no money for winning tournaments, even though she drew overflow crowds wherever she played. In decades past, the top female players usually came from well-to-do families, so getting a "piece of the action" was not important. But Lenglen was not wealthy, and she knew that as soon as her tennis career was over, she would have to give up the opulent lifestyle she was enjoying as the world's most celebrated player. In 1926, she renounced her amateur status and agreed to make a paid tour of the United States, thus becoming the sport's first professional. The experiment would prove a failure, although it did help men's pro tennis to get off the ground. Nevertheless, it was a watershed moment for women's sports.

In the years that followed, women's tennis became more and more of a power game. Helen Wills, a cold-blooded competitor who wore down opponents with her flawless baseline game, ruled the sport into the 1930s. "Little Miss Pokerface" was immensely popular with the press, which helped keep tennis alive and well during the early days of the Great Depression. Quiet and conservative, Wills was actually not very popular

Helen Wills dominated women's tennis for nearly a decade. Though she preferred to play from the baseline, she did not miss many opportunities at the net.

with the crowds. But her main rival, Helen Jacobs, was. She electrified spectators with her withering backhand and crisp volleys, and shocked the establishment by donning tennis shorts instead of a dress. Succeeding these two champions was Alice Marble, a tomboy from Northern California, who was the game's first serve-and-volley specialist. She advanced the power game significantly, and there is no telling what she might have accomplished had the Second World War not interrupted her career. Always anxious to find new challenges, Marble offered her services to the military, and became a spy during the war—putting her life on the line more than once to gather information from the Nazis.

In the years following the war, there were no significant advances in women's tennis. Although the overall quality of play improved, the top players were no better or worse than the stars of the 1920s and 30s. This opened the way for the game's first teenage superstar, Maureen Connolly, who in 1949 came out of California to win the national 18-and-under championship at the age of 14. Within two years, "Little Mo" was the U.S. champion, and a year after that she won Wimbledon. Ironically, she never really liked tennis. Her mother—a frustrated musician determined to have a famous daughter—pushed her into the sport after a botched tonsillectomy ruined Maureen's chances at a singing career.

Connolly spent an unprecedented amount of time practicing, spurred on by her mother and coach, both of whom told Maureen that opponents hated her because she was not like them. Thus her mom became the first in a long and unpleasant line of pathetic, overbearing tennis parents. In 1953, Connolly won all four Grand Slam Tournaments—the Australian, French and U.S. championships, and Wimbledon. No woman had ever done that before, and no one, it seemed, had the game to unseat Little Mo. Then, as quickly as she had rocketed to the top, her run ended. Sideswiped by a cement truck while riding her horse, she broke her leg and never returned to tennis.

Into this void stepped Althea Gibson, the first woman to move from the all-black American Tennis Association to the all-white USLTA circuit. She did so with the help of Alice Marble, who in 1950 penned an open letter to a major tennis magazine after Gibson was barred from competing at the U.S. championships in Forest Hills. "If Althea Gibson represents a challenge to the present crop of players," she wrote, "then it's only

Althea Gibson, the sport's first African-American superstar, was the top-ranked U.S. player in '57 and '58. Her tremendous reach made her a terror at the net.

fair that they meet this challenge on the courts." Gibson worked her way up the rankings, using her great strength and stamina to outlast opponents. In 1956, she broke through with her first Grand Slam win in France, and she took the U.S. title in 1957 and 1958.

Marble had a bigger hand in the development of the game's next great star, Billie Jean King. Marble began coaching Billie Jean (who then went by her maiden name, Moffitt) after she broke into the Top 20 at the age of 16. She tutored the teenager in the fine points of serve-and-volley tennis, and within a year she was ranked number four. King captured her first Grand Slam singles title in 1966 at Wimbledon, and won the prestigious tournament again five more times in the 1960s and 70s. She also won the U.S. title four times, and the French and Australian championships once each. King represented the pinnacle of female athletic achievement while she played. On the court, she was intense, aggressive and analytical—overwhelming her opponents when she had an edge and finding a way to win when she did not. Off the court, she approached life the same way. An outspoken proponent of women's rights, King had a keen understanding of how to make friends, coerce enemies, and use the media to achieve her goals.

In 1968, the longtime rule banning pros from competing in the major tournaments was abandoned, ushering in the modern era of professional (or "open") tennis. In 1970, King led a movement to get more prize money for women, whose earnings lagged far behind those of their male counterparts. The result was a landmark sponsorship deal with Virginia Slims, which sponsored the women's tour for more than two decades. A few years later she helped form the Women's Tennis Association (WTA),

Whether chasing down a lob or lobbying for equal prize money, Billie Jean King always gave everything she had. She was ranked in the Top Ten 17 times.

which still runs the pro tour. King also defeated self-proclaimed "male chauvinist pig" Bobby Riggs in a nationally televised "Battle of the Sexes" in 1973.

With more fans, more media attention, and more money, women's tennis blossomed in the 1970s. Billie Jean King and other veteran stars—including Margaret Court, Rosemary Casals and Francoise Durr—eventually gave way to a new generation of highly skilled competitors. This group featured England's Virginia Wade, Australia's Evonne Goolagong, Czechoslovakia's Martina Navratilova, and America's Chris Evert. It was Evert who in many ways defined women's tennis as it grew into a multi-million dollar industry. On the court she displayed the cool, measured efficiency of a champion, while off the court she had a girlish charm that captured the hearts of fans and the sports media alike. Evert and Navratilova battled like a couple of gladiators during the 1970s and well into the 80s, with each finding ways to raise her game a notch to keep up with the other.

In Chris and Martina's universe, women were no longer expected to uphold antiquated traditions and be "ladylike" when they competed—they were expected to leave everything they had out on the court. The young players who learned this lesson from Evert and Navratilova started to arrive by the end of the 1970s. They were impossibly young and incredibly tough, and their successes changed the way women's tennis was played, taught and operated, from the kiddie clinics all the way up to the pros. Tracy Austin, a cute little 14-year-old with the heart of an assassin, hit the WTA Tour after racking up a record 25 junior titles. She won her very first professional tournament and cracked the Top 10 within a year. In 1979, at the age of 16, Austin won the U.S. Open, grabbed the number one spot, and was named *Associated Press* Female Athlete of the Year. To many, the women's game was approaching an incomprehensible crossroads. Could it be that 17-year-olds were in their prime and 25-year-olds were "over the hill?" It seemed to defy logic.

The women's game had indeed taken a dramatic turn. One teen sensation after another hit the pros during the 1980s and 90s, with Jennifer Capriati joining the tour at the age of 13 in 1989. It got to the point where, if a player was still competing in 18-and-under tournaments past the age of 16, she was actually considered to be an unsuitable prospect for the pro tour! In this brave new world, some young stars went on to bigger and better things, while others flamed out. The following chapters take a look at some of the players who brought the sport into the 1990s, and a few who will bring it into the next century.

Martina Navratilova won a record 1,438 singles matches during her career. She and archrival Chris Evert dominated the game for more than 15 years, winning a combined total of 324 tournaments.

"Some people have dreams when they are four years old, but I'm making my dreams now."

Lindsay Davenport

S ometimes life seems like an endless series of adjustments. Lindsay Davenport certainly feels that way. As a kid she had to get used to tennis while being raised in a volleyball-crazy family. As a teenager she had to change her game when she shot up over six feet tall. And as a young woman she has had to adjust to the on- and off-court demands of being a Top 10 player. But as Lindsay sees it, there is nothing wrong with changing course—as long as you're the one doing the navigating. "If I had to title my autobiography, I would call it *Driving Into the Night*," she laughs. "I'm not sure where I'm going, and I can't always see what obstacles lay ahead, but I'm the one driving."

Although Lindsay's life has had its twists and turns, she never lacked direction. She and her sisters, Leiann and Shannon, grew up in Palos Verdes, California. Their parents were very active in volleyball. Her father Wink, in fact, was a member of the 1968 Olympic team. Soon that became the family sport. Lindsay found tennis around the age of seven, and was immediately drawn to it. That was fine with her mom and dad, who had always hoped their kids would find other sports to their liking.

The tough thing for the Davenports, of course, was to resist the temptation to start coaching. Luckily this was not a problem—from the moment Lindsay picked up a racket, she seemed to know exactly what to do with it. She could watch an opponent, analyze her game, and then formulate a strategy to win. Tennis people were blown away by this ability. There are a lot of players on the pro tour who can't do that!

Behind Lindsay's easy manner is one of the game's keenest analytical minds.

Self-conscious about her size as a teenager, Lindsay has turned her 6' 2" frame into a source of awesome power.

As Lindsay entered her teenage years, she began to grow faster than the other girls in the junior ranks. There were even whispers that her height might one day work against her. It is very difficult to develop a consistent game when your arms, legs and torso are getting longer every month. And girls often feel self-conscious about their height at this age. Lindsay tripped over her own feet from time to time, but ultimately she was able to make the physical adjustments. And she learned to deal with the mental challenges of being the tallest girl on the court. "I'm OK with it now, but I wouldn't have minded being a couple inches shorter," she admits. "I mean, you can't wear heels, but there are other things to life than pumps."

Among those "other things" was being the top young player in the United States. Lindsay reached that level at the age of 15, when she captured the 18-and-under singles and doubles titles in 1991. By 1992, her awkward moments on the court were few and far between, and she had learned to enhance her analytical skills with the raw power generated by her 6' 2" frame. After Lindsay won the 1993 Junior U.S. Open, it was time to make a decision: should she turn pro, or remain an amateur and continue to roll over less-talented opponents?

What made Lindsay's choice especially difficult was that she loved school. She was a straight-A student at Murrieta Valley High, and had long assumed that the combination of her classroom and tennis skills would get her into any college in the country. Now the timetable had been pushed up. In the end, the lure of competing against the best players in the world led Lindsay to choose the pro circuit. She truly believed she could beat the best, and there was only one way to find out.

One week after turning pro, Lindsay defeated Gabriela Sabatini, the number five player in the world. A short time later Lindsay won the European Open. By sea-

Getting Personal

Lindsay was born in Palo Verdes, California on June 8, 1976...During her big 1992 junior season, Lindsay was nicknamed "Bagel" because she beat so many opponents 6-0, 6-0... She credits her success in doubles to the teamwork her parents taught her. Her partners say it is because she has such an analytical mind...Lindsay keeps her tennis trophies in her garage, and her Olympic medal in her mother's sock drawer...Lindsay is one of only seven players to defeat both Steffi Graf and Martina Hingis while they held the number one world ranking...Lindsay is just a shade under 6' 3". She wears a men's size 10 Nike tennis shoe.

son's end, she was ranked in the Top 20 and *Tennis* magazine named her Rookie of the Year. Although she was just a kid, Lindsay adjusted to the demands of the WTA Tour like a seasoned veteran. Rather than "hitting the wall," after her first season, she continued to progress. In 1994, she became the first American woman in three years to crack the Top 10. And in 1995 she battled through injuries to win one singles title and four doubles championships with four different partners.

Lindsay's "coming out party" took place at the 1996 Olympics, in Atlanta. Given little chance of winning a medal, she went almost unnoticed as she knocked off one top player after another to advance to the finals. There Lindsay defeated Arantxa Sanchez Vicario to win one of the

Career Highlights	
Year	**Achievement**
1991	Tennis Magazine Junior Player of the Year
1992	U.S. Junior Singles and Doubles Champion
1996	French Open Doubles Champion
1996	Olympic Gold Medalist
1997	U.S. Hardcourt Champion
1997	U.S. Open Doubles Champion

most surprising gold medals of the Summer Games. "My mom and my sister, Leiann, were crying real hard, and my other sister, Shannon, was real happy," she remembers. "My dad was also really happy. They said, 'Oh, we're so proud of you' and 'You're awesome.' That was definitely the most proud I've ever been in my life, not only for myself but for my family and my country."

Lindsay broke into the Top 5 right after the Olympics, and capped off her incredible year by winning the WTA doubles championship with Mary Jo Fernandez. Since then, Lindsay—who sometimes seemed to shy away from big matches—has developed quite an appetite for tournament victories. Her 1997 resume included seven more doubles titles and six singles crowns. Early in 1998, she outdueled Martina Hingis to win the Pan Pacific Open, marking the first time she had defeated the sport's top player in a tournament final. What most impressed tennis watchers about Lindsay's rise to prominence was that she seemed to add a new wrinkle to her game each and every week. Indeed, she had discovered one of the keys to becoming a champion: win or lose, take something from your experience and learn how to use it in your next event.

In Lindsay's mind, she still has plenty to learn. She knows, for instance, that improving her footwork will enable her to come to the net more often—and that is where she can use her fantastic wingspan to put away balls that others on the tour cannot even reach. She also works tirelessly on her groundstrokes, knowing that hitting the ball deeper will give her more opportunities to rush the net.

Ultimately, Lindsay realizes that making a serious run at the number-one slot will come down to the mental aspects of the game. And she has a pretty clear road map of what that will entail. "I'm trying to eliminate the highs and lows that go with constantly competing," Lindsay says. "I'm also trying to become more comfortable in the spotlight. Keeping my emotions on a more even keel helps me keep the tennis in perspective. I've grown up a lot and don't want to settle for just a Top 10 ranking my whole career. I want to give tennis my all and see where it takes me."

Lindsay collected plenty of hardware in 1997, winning 13 singles and doubles championships. That October, she became the top-ranked doubles player in the world.

ON HER MIND

"I have never set any specific goals.
I just want to play my best tennis."

Steffi Graf

To be successful at something, you often have to start from the "ground floor" and work your way up. Steffi Graf started even lower than that. Her first tennis matches took place in the family basement, where her father tied a length of twine between two chairs and marked out a tiny court. There four-year-old Steffi, using a sawed-off racket, played Peter Graf for the ultimate prize: ice cream with strawberries on top. While Steffi was concentrating on dessert, her dad had bigger things in mind. So convinced was he that Steffi had the talent to be a tennis star that he quit his job as an insurance salesman and opened his own tennis club near their home in Mannheim, West Germany.

With her father acting as full-time coach, Steffi progressed rapidly. At the age of six she won her first junior tournament, and when she turned 10 Peter took her to work with famed coach Boris Breskvar. By age 13, Steffi had won the German 18-and-unders and established herself as the finest young player in the country. After that, there was nothing left to accomplish in junior tennis. With the support of her parents, Steffi joined the women's pro tour. Within two years she was playing deep into Grand Slam tournaments, and saw her ranking climb steadily toward the Top 25. She also won a gold medal in the 1984 Olympics, at which tennis was a demonstration sport.

By the mid-1980s, Steffi was being proclaimed the heiress to the throne that had been occupied for so many years by legends Martina Navratilova and Chris Evert. Steffi's coming of age, in fact, occurred at the 1986 Family Circle Cup, when she defeated Evert to win the tournament.

Steffi's victory at the 1996 Chase Championships marked the fifth time she won the big season-ending tournament.

Players who test Steffi's backhand are courting disaster. She can slice it down the line, roll it crosscourt, or bang it past an opponent charging the net.

In all, Steffi won eight events in 1986 and reached the finals of three others. That began an amazing streak, during which the rising star advanced to the final round in 21 consecutive tournaments. In 1987, Steffi won the French Open for her first Grand Slam singles title, and finished the season as the WTA's top-ranked player. In 1988, she erased any doubt as to her status as the new queen of women's tennis when she won all four Grand Slam events. There she capped off a great year by winning the gold medal at the Olympics in South Korea.

Steffi was an amazing young player. She was agile, cunning, and enormously talented. She used the whole court, hit her forehand like a cannon shot, and developed what is traditionally the weakest part of a player's arsenal—the backhand—into a most formidable weapon. The only problem was that Steffi had no one to challenge her. Evert and Navratilova were nearing the end of their careers, and the new up-and-coming players at the time did not have power or stamina enough to beat Steffi. Indeed, from 1988 to 1990 she won eight of nine Grand Slam events, and from June of '89 to May of '90 she won an incredible 66 matches in a row. Steffi not only beat her opponents, she blew them off the court—often winning 6-0, 6-0. "I like to get things done fast," she explains, "win points and matches as quickly as I can."

Every great tennis player needs another great player to challenge her. For Steffi, that was hard-hitting Monica Seles, who burst on to the scene in 1990. Starting with that year's French Open, Seles won eight of the next 12 Grand Slam singles titles. In 1991 and '92, Seles took away from Steffi the number one ranking, which had belonged to her since August of 1987. Seles also won most of their head-to-head battles. Soon there were whispers that Steffi was "slipping"—that at the age of 23 she was "getting old." The very notion was absurd, of course, and no one knew this more than Steffi. She worked hard to sharpen her game, and devised new ways to counter Monica's power. Steffi believed that 1993 would be her year.

Getting Personal

Steffi was born on June 14, 1969, in Bruhl, Germany...Her brother's name is Michael...In her spare time Steffi has worked as a fashion model and as a photographer...Steffi takes her place in tennis very seriously. "I feel a moral responsibility to help the game maintain its standards and integrity," she says. "I hope I give back to the public what they give to me."...Though Steffi looks cool and unemotional on the court, she is extremely sensitive...In 1995, Steffi became the first player ever to win each of the four Grand Slams at least four times...Her 1996 Wimbledon victory was her 100th career tournament championship...Steffi was named ITF world champion for the seventh time in 1996.

As it turned out, Steffi would win back the top spot—but not at all in the way that she wanted. On April 30, at a tournament in Germany, a spectator stabbed Seles in the back. It was revealed later that the man was a deranged fan who worshiped Steffi, and could not bear the thought that Seles had usurped her number-one ranking. It would take her two years to start playing tennis again. During that time, Steffi once again dominated the WTA Tour. She won 10 tournaments in 1993, seven in 1994, nine in 1995 and seven in 1996. She won the French Open, Wimbledon and the U.S. Open twice each in '95 and '96. And in 1997 Steffi became only the second woman to surpass $20 million in career earnings. Her

Career Highlights

Achievement	Years
WTA Most Improved Player	1986
French Open Singles Champion	1987, 1988, 1993, 1995, 1996
WTA Player of the Year	1987, 1988, 1989, 1990, 1993, 1994, 1995, 1996
Wimbledon Doubles Champion	1988
Olympic Gold Medalist	1988
Wimbledon Singles Champion	1988, 1989, 1991, 1992, 1993, 1995, 1996
U.S. Open Singles Champion	1988, 1989, 1993, 1995, 1996
Australian Open Singles Champion	1988, 1989, 1990, 1994

off-court endorsements pushed her total income past the $100 million mark. Not surprisingly, by this time some experts were saying that Steffi was the finest player in history.

Yet despite her success, these were not happy years for Steffi. In 1995, the German government concluded an investigation into her business affairs, which had long been handled by her father. Peter Graf was accused of failing to pay more than $10 million in taxes, and despite his adamant claims to the contrary, Steffi was suspected of being in on the scam. Worried that Peter might leave the country before he went to trial, the German government held him in prison. As if this were not enough to deal with, Steffi's back was beginning to ache constantly, and she had surgery to remove a bone spur from her left foot. To make matters even worse, reporters, camera crews and photographers seemed to be waiting for her wherever she went.

Somehow Steffi managed to shut out the pain and continue her masterful tennis. At the end of the 1996 season she celebrated her eighth year as the WTA's top-ranked player. But whereas Steffi had always had the bounce and spirit of a teenager, she now had the grim, humorless focus of a war veteran. In a funny way, though, this made her appreciate tennis more than ever. "When you're 17," she says, "you win and you win and you just accept it."

Injuries diminished Steffi's effectiveness early in the 1997 season, and after dropping to third in the rankings (her lowest level since the mid-1980s), she decided to have her left knee surgically repaired and sit out the rest of the year. She wanted to regroup, recover, and spend more time with her dad.

As the 1998 season began, Steffi worked hard to regain her past form. Some say she can do it. Others believe she will leave tennis if she cannot. If Steffi does come back 100 percent, she will be doing battle with some tough, young newcomers. Of course, that is just the kind of challenge she needs to spur her on to new heights. Should Steffi choose to retire, she will do so with more than 100 career tournament victories and 374 weeks as the world's top-ranked player—more than any man or woman in the history of the sport.

In her second tournament after returning from surgery, Steffi reached the semifinals of the 1998 Evert Cup before an injury forced her to bow out.

ON HER MIND

"I like everything about tennis; the game, the courts, the competition, and doing everything you can to win. It's such a beautiful sport."

Martina Hingis

Martina Hingis does not mind being underestimated. In fact, she prefers her opponents to take her lightly. It makes it easier to beat them. And more satisfying. Looking at Martina from across the net, it is totally understandable how other players could think they have a chance: she is of average size, boasts average groundstrokes, her serve is nothing to brag about, she does not move all that well, and has yet to develop anything like a "game face." So how do you explain that Martina is already the youngest winner of a Grand Slam singles title in this century, and the first woman in any sport to earn $3 million in a season?

It's all in the mind, as they say. No one on the WTA Tour is a better strategist, no one processes information quicker, and no one plays (and wins) mind games the way Martina does. "The strongest part of my game is in my head," agrees Martina. "I play what I feel. I respond to the ball. It comes from my whole body. The rhythm and the timing are much more important to me than power. I never had power. I needed something else. Instead I had to be smart. I had to think until my head broke."

Martina was practically born to be a tennis star. Her mother, Melanie Molitor, was a tennis pro in her native Czechoslovakia. She named her child after Martina Navratilova, the country's most famous player. Martina was two and a half when she first gripped a racket, and from that day forward her mother made sure that the sport maintained its grip on her.

Melanie made tennis fun. Instead of boring drills, she came up with games that would develop Martina's skills and challenge her creativity. By

Media darling Martina meets the press after winning the 1998 Australian Open.

Thanks to her great anticipation, there are few shots Martina cannot return.

the time she was a teenager, she had spent as much time working out her brain as she had her body. Martina delighted in outsmarting bigger, stronger girls. She could work a point so that an opponent would never be able to hit her best shot, and lull her into playing to Martina's strengths. Martina so frustrated other players that they ended up making tons of unforced errors—and rarely did they understand what was happening until well after the match was done.

Martina's parents were divorced when she was four years old, and she rarely saw her father. In 1988 her mother and new stepfather, Andreas, decided that it was time to leave the country. The break-up of the Soviet Union had begun and the political situation in Eastern Bloc nations was becoming increasingly unstable. Melanie and Andreas decided that for Martina's tennis career to continue, they had to flee Czechoslovakia. They ended up moving to Switzerland.

There Martina thrived. In 1989, at the age of 9, she won the Swiss 12-and-under championships. In the spring of 1993, at the age of 12, Martina won the French Open junior title, negotiating her way through a draw filled with talented 17- and 18-year-olds. No one her age had ever captured a Grand Slam junior tournament. At 13, she won the Wimbledon and French junior championships. By the time Martina was 14, she was as good as many of the players on the professional level. Her mother would have liked her to play a few more years on the junior circuit, but a new rule was about to go into effect which would bar players under the age of 18 from playing professionally. Feeling she had no choice, Martina registered as a pro and joined the WTA Tour.

Getting Personal

Martina was born on September 30, 1980...She began competing in tournaments at the age of four...Martina believes that if she plans carefully and executes properly, there is no reason she cannot win every point...Though named after Martina Navratilova, Martina says the player she most admires is Hall of Famer Chris Evert...She is determined not to let tennis overwhelm her, and tries to be as "normal" as possible. During the '97 Australian Open, she was spotted rollerblading around the tennis compound...Martina owns two horses— Sorrenta and Montana—and has ridden them in competition...She also owns a German Shepherd named Zorro.

Martina entered the Australian Open in January of 1995 and became the youngest player to win a match in the event during the Open Era. By the time she turned 15 that season, she had already pocketed $1 million in prize money. But not all was rosy with Martina and her mother. Melanie explained that, because tennis was now Martina's job, she would have to take it more seriously. That meant longer workouts and better conditioning. At first, Martina resisted. She detested practicing. But soon she came around to her mom's way of thinking. In time, she doubled her daily practice time and added aerobics and shadow-boxing to her training regimen. "It was a turning point," she admits.

Career *Highlights*

Year	Achievement
1987	Czech 9-And-Under Singles Champion
1991	European 16-And-Under Singles Champion
1994	European 18-And-Under Singles Champion
1994	ITF Junior Girls Singles Champion
1994	Wimbledon Junior Singles Champion
1995	WTA Most Impressive Newcomer
1996	Wimbledon Doubles Champion
1996	WTA Most Improved Player
1997	Australian Open Singles and Doubles Champion
1997	Hilton Head Singles and Doubles Champion
1997	Wimbledon Singles Champion
1997	U.S. Open Singles Champion
1997	WTA Player of the Year
1998	Australian Open Singles Champion
1998	French Open Doubles Champion

Indeed it was—both for Martina and for women's tennis. She rose quickly up the rankings, ambushing one Top 10 player after another on an unstoppable drive toward the number one slot. Martina broke into the Top 20 in 1995, just 15 months after debuting at number 399. She also excelled in doubles, becoming the youngest winner of a Grand Slam championship when she took the 1996 Wimbledon title with Helena Sukova. In January of 1997, she scored her first Grand Slam singles victory at the Australian Open, then won at Wimbledon and the U.S. Open to gain a stranglehold on the top spot in the WTA rankings. With veterans Steffi Graf and Monica Seles dominating everyone else during the 1990s and a lack of charismatic young stars, women's tennis desperately needed a new champion like Martina.

With her amazing 1997 season, Martina energized the WTA Tour and got people saying positive things about women's tennis for the first time in a long time. No one was talking anymore about the comeback of Monica Seles, Steffi Graf's tax troubles, or Jennifer Capriati's burnout. Instead, the buzz was about Martina—and which young players would rise to challenge her.

Though it may be too early to say for sure, Martina does appear to have the qualities that will keep her in the headlines for years to come. Her game, which is already superb, actually seems to be improving. On the court, she inspires crowds with poise and savvy well beyond her years. Off the court, she amazes sportswriters with her precocious remarks. Among her many interesting comments, Martina has stated that she means more to tennis than Tiger Woods means to golf. At an awards banquet held less than two weeks after she claimed the top spot in women's tennis, she was asked to announce the Player of the Year. When she opened the envelope she feigned surprise and said, "There must be some mistake—it doesn't say *me*."

When Martina's competitors hear her patting herself on the back or read her quotes in the

Even on the most basic shots, Martina is always a study in focus and concentration.

newspaper, they probably want to strangle her. But who's to say that is not part of her overall strategy? After all, the more opponents want to beat Martina, the easier it is to make them beat themselves. It is a little scary to think about, but every time she brags to reporters or giggles for the cameras she may actually be setting up her next opponent!

ON HER MIND

"I'm playing for the fans...whenever they come and ask for autographs I always try to give it to everybody...I'm out there for the people."

Anna Kournikova

Many girls fantasize about being rich, beautiful and famous when they grow up. But what if you realized that dream by the age of 16? How would you handle it? That is the question Anna Kournikova must answer every day. Though only a teenager, she is already worth millions of dollars, her face graces the covers of magazines worldwide, and many regard her as the next superstar in women's tennis. Anna is a sex symbol, a world-class athlete and a rock 'n roll princess all rolled up into one. What could be better than that? For now, nothing. In fact, she is having a blast. Anna courts fame and craves attention; she savors every bit that comes her way, and she makes no bones about it.

This is nothing new. The process began for Anna nearly a decade ago, when Russian tennis fans started hearing about a little girl who hit like a seasoned pro. Anna grew up in Moscow and began playing tennis at her youth club sometime after her fifth birthday. By the time she was eight, her parents realized they might have a future world-class player on their hands. Her father, Sergei, worked for the Russian Physical Culture Ministry, so he was able to place Anna in an accelerated tennis program at the Spartak Club.

Soon everyone in Moscow knew about her, including several Russian-born NHL hockey players. Through them, word of Anna filtered to the International Management Group, the most powerful sports representation agency in the United States. In 1991, at the age of 10, Anna became IMG's youngest client. In February of 1992, Anna and her mother, Alla,

Anna had reason to celebrate in 1997, when she became the first woman in the Open Era to reach the semifinals in her Wimbledon debut.

Anna's serve is a major part of her arsenal. It helped her score her first career victory over Martina Hingis, at the 1998 German Open.

moved to Florida so she could be coached by Nick Bollettieri, who had trained Monica Seles, Andre Agassi and several other stars.

Bollettieri was astounded at how advanced Anna's game was. He quickly realized that his biggest challenge would be holding her back. Anna hungered to win, and saw little reason why she should have to hit with the other students at the Bollettieri Academy. She would disrupt teaching sessions and demand special instruction, or smash winners past the players with whom she was supposed to be practicing. Anna felt that it was stupid to train when she could be playing matches instead, because that is when she was at her best.

In 1995, 13-year-old Anna was finally unleashed on junior tennis. She possessed great shot-making ability and a super net game, and that was enough to make her the most feared player on the junior circuit. She won everything in sight that summer, including the prestigious Orange Bowl 18-and-under title. Among her other 1995 championships were the Italian Open junior title and European 18-and-unders. At season's end Anna, just 14, was crowned junior world champion.

In October of 1995, Anna turned pro. She joined the WTA Tour for her first full season a few months later, and slowly worked her way up the rankings. She captured her first pro tournament in Midland, Michigan and beat Top 20 stars Amanda Coetzer and Barbara Paulus on her way to winning the WTA's Newcomer of the Year award. Anna even got to play for Russia in the Federation Cup, and won a match against Switzerland, becoming the youngest ever to do so.

As the 1997 season began, Anna had the confidence, the net skills and the groundstrokes to win consistently on

Getting Personal

Anna was born in Moscow on June 7, 1981...She considers her mother her best friend and number one coach...Anna's father still lives and works in Moscow, but he visits his wife and daughter four or five times a year...Her first success at Wimbledon came in 1995, when she reached the semis of the junior tournament...Anna loves Madonna. "It's unbelievable how she's always changing and stays in the spotlight," she says...To those who accuse her of paying too much attention to the way she looks, Anna replies, "I think that tennis is a lady's sport, so we should look out there like ladies. I just try to look after myself and really play."

the pro tour. All she lacked was power. She and Bollettieri worked hard to introduce this element to her game. He knew that all of the other pieces were already there. By mid-summer, Anna had added more "oomph" to her attack. She had learned to hit the ball on the rise, which added more speed to her shots and gave her opponents less time to react. With Wimbledon approaching, Anna felt she was ready to make her first big move as a pro.

The odds were not with her. In fact, only one player making her Wimbledon debut during the Open Era had ever gotten past the quarter-finals, and that was Chris Evert. The tournament is played on grass, a surface unfamiliar to most young players, and the pressure of performing in

Career *Highlights*

Year	Achievement
1995	Orange Bowl Singles Champion
1995	European 18-And-Under Singles Champion
1995	Italian Open Junior SIngles Champion
1996	Youngest Federation Cup Player in History
1996	Russian Olympic Team Member
1996	WTA Most Impressive Newcomer
1997	Wimbledon Singles Semifinalist
1998	Lipton Singles Finalist

the sport's most hallowed event can be overwhelming. But as the first week unfolded, it was Anna who was doing the overwhelming. With the British crowds cheering her every point and the British press chronicling her every footstep, she took down one opponent after another with her marvelous all-court attack. The first big player she beat was Germany's Anke Huber. In the quarterfinals, Anna upset Croatian star Iva Majoli, who had just won the French Open. Not until she faced Martina Hingis in the semis did Anna's remarkable run come to an end.

A foot injury ended Anna's season early, but on the whole it had been a remarkable success. To her added power she added consistency—a rare commodity for a player so young. Tennis experts took special note that Anna did not lose to a single player ranked lower than number 15, and eight of her 10 losses in 1997 were to Top 10 stars.

In March of 1998, *Sports Illustrated* ran a feature story on Anna. It appeared during the Lipton Championships, which is one of the biggest tournaments of the year. With sports fans all over the country now watching to see how she would do, Anna went through her half of the draw with the cool, brutal efficiency of a trained killer, picking off one high-profile player after another. After wiping out young Mirjana Lucic—who may soon be ascending the rankings herself—Anna disposed of Top 10 stars

Monica Seles, Conchita Martinez, Lindsay Davenport and Arantxa Sanchez Vicario to reach the final. There she met Venus Williams.

In what is likely to be the first of many final-round showdowns between the two tennis prodigies, Anna blew Williams away in the first set 6-2, and barely lost the second set 6-4. She ran out of gas in the third, however, and watched as her rival pulled away to take the coveted Lipton crown. To say that their match had the tennis world abuzz would be a major understatement. It was the best showing either player had ever made up to that time. That they did it at the heralded Lipton (instead of some out-of-the-way event) was even more exciting.

For Anna, however, playing well was not much consolation. A year or two ago, the adoring fans and the media attention would have been enough. But not anymore. She hated walking off that court with a loss. That is not what the other players on the tour like to hear.

An unknown at the 1997 Australian Open, Anna was the hottest autograph in Melbourne when she returned in 1998.

They knew Anna would begin to develop a taste for championships...they were just hoping she would be happy staying a kid a little while longer.

ON HER MIND

"I'm calm. I'm so happy. Of course, I'm glad I'm winning, but it's not like it means everything. I'm healthy. Everything in my life is good."

Mary Pierce

Every father wants the best for his daughter. But when a father *demands* his daughter be the best, it can lead to trouble. That, in a nutshell, is the story of Mary Pierce. For a long time, in fact, it looked as if she might be the tragic victim of history's all-time worst "tennis dad." Luckily for Mary, an unhappy tale had a happy ending.

It is not unusual in the world of tennis for parents to cross the line from coach to critic. Young players sometimes need a kick in the pants from the people they love most. Jim Pierce, however, went way past that point. When Mary won—and she won often as a junior—Jim often took the credit; when she lost, he directed the blame at his daughter. He would belittle Mary when she made a mistake and insult her opponents when they beat her. He was abusive and disruptive, and an embarrassment to tennis. It got so bad that Jim Pierce was actually barred from many tournaments, and finally Mary had to seek legal help to keep him away.

When Mary's mother, Yannick, met and married Jim Pierce, there was no hint of the troubles to come. She did not know that her husband had committed several serious crimes in the late 1950s, or that he had once escaped from jail. And Jim never let on that he had been diagnosed with mental problems while an inmate in a psychiatric prison. Mary and her younger brother, David, grew up in an atmosphere of emotional terror and physical abuse—she once described her dad as being like Dr. Jekyll and Mr. Hyde.

Mary could not have been more pleased with her fast start in 1998, as she won three of her first five tournaments.

Mary's concentration has served her well, both on and off the court.

At the age of 10, Mary was introduced to tennis by her father. Jim realized his daughter was an exceptional athlete, and believed that she had the talent to become a pro. Unfortunately, he also became her coach. Mary was taught to hit everything as hard as she could, leaving little margin for error. On most days, she was able to over-whelm her opponent. But when she was a little off—or when another player was able to disrupt her tim-ing—her shots sailed long or into the net. Naturally, this infuriated Jim. According to Mary that is when the rough stuff began. "He would slap me after I lost a match or sometimes just if I had had a bad practice," she remembers. "When I told my mom, that would cause fights, too. So sometimes you're afraid to say anything because of that."

Despite the unimaginable pressure, Mary continued to develop her game. But as she worked her way up the junior ladder, she became increasingly distracted and embarrassed by her dad. He would berate her from the stands and scream insults at other players. Mary understood on some level that what he was doing had a positive aspect ("One of the few justifiable reasons for his behavior was that he wanted to make me men-tally tougher," she claims), but by this time it was threatening to derail her promising career. In 1987, when Mary was 12, Jim was banned from all events by the Florida Tennis Association. In 1989, the USTA dropped

Mary from its player development program, feeling Jim Pierce had simply become too difficult to control. Undaunted, he decided Mary should turn professional. This horrified many tennis fans—no American girl her age had ever joined the tour so young.

Jim's behavior got even worse as Mary embarked upon her pro career, yet somehow Mary managed to get better. She won a couple of small tournaments in 1989, '90 and '91, and advanced to the fourth round of the 1992 French Open to break into the Top 20. Yet even that moment was ruined by her dad, who got into a fistfight in the stands. Incredibly, as Mary enjoyed more success on the WTA Tour, the incidents involving Jim seemed to multiply. At the 1993 French Open he choked Mary's cousin, whom he felt was distracting her as they watched a future opponent play. During her third-round match, Jim launched into a

Getting Personal

Mary was born on January 15, 1975...In her first junior tournament she beat the top-seeded player on court 13. That has been her lucky number ever since...In 1986, when Mary was 11, her father sold the family house, pulled the kids out of school, and began traveling from tournament to tournament, living out of the family car...Mary's pro debut at 14 years, two months was a record for U.S. women until Jennifer Capriati joined the tour in 1990 at age 13...After being dropped by the USTA in 1989, Mary became a French national so that she could receive funding and coaching from France's junior tennis program. She has competed internationally for France ever since—including at the 1992 and '96 Olympics...Mary does not think of the "French Connection" as having much bearing on who she is. "I don't see why I have to be French or American," she says. "I feel like a little of both." She actually holds passports from Canada, France and the U.S...Mary finished 1997 ranked number 7 and was voted WTA Comeback Player of the Year...Mary was the first Frenchwoman to win a Grand Slam title since Francoise Durr won at Roland Garros in 1967...She donated her racket from the 1995 Australian final to a charity auction benefiting the victims of the earthquake in Kobe, Japan...Entering the 1998 season, Mary was one of only seven players to defeat both Martina Hingis and Steffi Graf...Mary led France to its first ever Federation Cup in 1997.

Career *Highlights*

Year	Achievement
1994	French Open Singles Finalist
1995	Australian Open Singles Champion
1997	Australian Open Singles Finalist
1997	Italian Open Singles Champion
1997	Federation Cup Champion

tirade and had to be removed from the stadium. After that he was banned from tournaments, and his picture was even posted in ticket booths in case he tried to sneak in as a fan. Finally, Mary had some control over her life.

"It was always Mary Pierce and her father did this, or Mary Pierce and her father did that," she says. "Now it's just Mary Pierce."

Mary knew how to play, but at this stage of her career she did not know how to *win*. With her father no longer able to coach her, she hired Nick Bollettieri, and he worked wonders with her. At the season-ending Virginia Slims Championships, she beat Gabriela Sabatini and Martina Navratilova (the first Top 10 players she had ever defeated), and rode that momentum into the next season. At the 1994 French Open she clobbered her opponents, including the usually awe-inspiring Steffi Graf, who watched in awe as Mary put away one shot after another. Only a case of nerves in the final against crafty Arantxa Sanchez Vicario kept Mary from taking her first Grand Slam. That would come at the beginning of the 1995 campaign, when she won the Australian Open.

Since then Mary has continued to sharpen her game. More important, though, she has come to grips with her past and begun to see her future in a new way. She is happy how her life turned out, and everyone on the tour has taken notice. No one deserves success more than Mary, and no one has gone through more to achieve it. She has even sought to patch up her relationship with her dad, whom she still credits with some of her success. The bottom line is that, for the first time, she can afford to relax and not to take things too seriously. "I think fun is the main word," Mary confirms. "My life off the court has changed. I'm feeling good inside, so I guess it shows on the outside too."

Mary's all-out effort helped the French team take the Federation Cup in 1997. It marked the first time that France had ever won the prestigious competition.

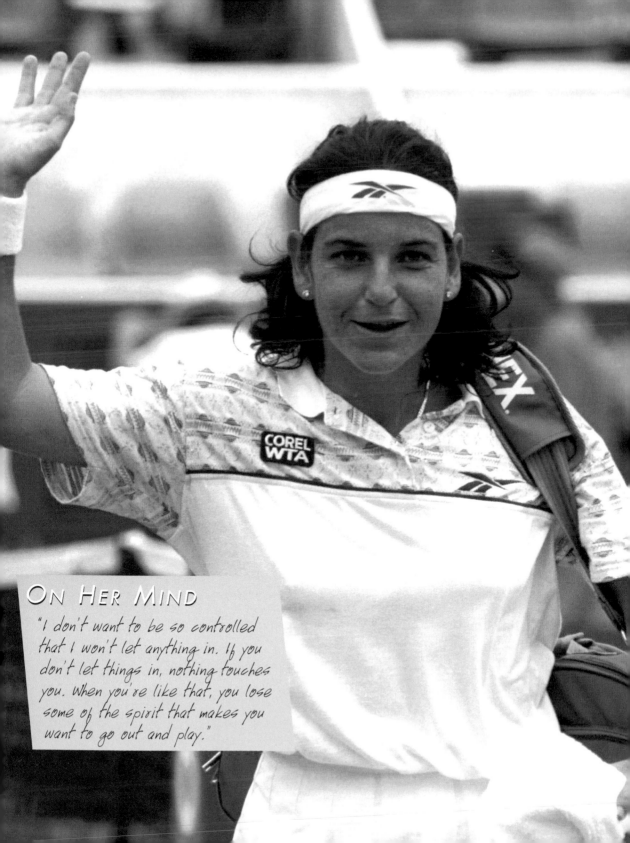

ON HER MIND

"I don't want to be so controlled that I won't let anything in. If you don't let things in, nothing touches you. When you're like that, you lose some of the spirit that makes you want to go out and play."

Arantxa Sanchez Vicario

The next time your little brother or sister wants to tag along when you go to the tennis courts, think twice before you say no. When Arantxa Sanchez Vicario was two years old, she used to go with Marisa, Emilio and Javier whenever they played at the local park in Barcelona, Spain. Eventually their dad, Emilio, Sr., got tired of Arantxa wandering onto the court and handed her a racket. The toddler never let that old Slazenger go—she even slept with it!

At the age of three, Arantxa was rallying against a backboard; by her eighth birthday she had already begun wearing her trademark ball holder; and in 1985, at the age of 13, she was the top player in her country. Arantxa achieved this distinction the same way she would accomplish everything in her tennis life: by never giving up. If she was hopelessly behind in a match, she would just dig in and come back one point at a time. If her best shots were not working, she would invent new ones on the spot. And win or lose, she never stopped smiling.

Perhaps that was because her future seemed to be so clear. Arantxa's plan was to gain experience in the juniors and earn a scholarship to an American university, just as sister Marisa had. With any luck, she might even have a pro career. Little did she know that her father had no intention of letting her leave. He missed Marisa desperately, and vowed to keep his younger daughter closer to home.

Arantxa beat Serena and Venus Williams to win her first event of 1998, the Sydney International.

Arantxa is a nightmare to play. She has the talent and imagination to produce clean winners from anywhere on the court.

Of course, he did not count on one thing: by the age of 14, Arantxa was clearly good enough to hold her own against the pros. The family got together to discuss the situation and everyone agreed that the best plan was for Arantxa to join the women's tour, with her mother traveling at her side.

In her first professional tournament, Arantxa won her first three matches. A few months later, she took the court against the great Martina Navratilova and nearly beat her. Over the next two seasons Arantxa increased her footspeed, anticipation and stamina, and added a wicked forehand to her arsenal. Suddenly, the fearless 16-year-old was more than just a "scrappy" player—she was becoming the player people most hated to play.

Arantxa's game was most effective on clay surfaces, where the ball slows down when it hits the ground. The French Open, which has always been played on clay, was the Grand Slam tournament she felt she could win. She had made it to the quarterfinals at Roland Garros in 1987 and 1988, so in 1989 she set her sights on knocking off Steffi Graf, who had won the event both years. She believed the key to beating Graf—who had won her last five Grand Slam finals—was mental, not physical. Arantxa knew that other players went into their matches with Steffi assuming they were going to lose. Arantxa decided to send a message and go right at her. She also followed Emilio's advice and kept the ball away from Graf's vaunted backhand. The strategy worked to perfection, as Arantxa took the first set in a thrilling tiebreaker, lost the second set, then outhustled the German superstar to win the final set, 7-5. At 17 years old, Arantxa was the youngest-ever French Open champ.

After her victory in Paris, Arantxa was no longer the unknown trying to ambush the top players. She was now top player doing whatever it took to stay there. Anyone in sports will tell you that it is a lot easier to reach the top than to remain there, and Arantxa is the only player on the tour from 1989

Getting Personal

Arantxa was born on December 18, 1971, in Madrid, Spain...her family moved to Barcelona when Arantxa was a young girl...her mother wanted the kids to take up skiing, but her father convinced her that tennis was a better sport...Arantxa is pronounced "Aran-cha" and is derived from the name of a Basque saint...In 1989, Arantxa added Vicario (her mother's maiden name) to her own, so that everyone could see their names in the paper when she won...After winning the French Open, Arantxa even got to meet the King and Queen of Spain...Arantxa's nickname is the "Barcelona Bumblebee"...She has two Yorkshire terriers named Roland and Garros, after the site of her first Grand Slam title...Arantxa stays very active with charity work. She is a celebrity chairperson of the Children's Cancer Research in Spain, and raises funds for Enriqueta Vilavecchia, which helps terminally ill children in her home country...She speaks six languages: Spanish, French, German, English, Italian, and her native Catalan...She has switched coaches eight times since turning pro. Her present coach is brother Emilio...her sister, Marisa, is a sports reporter for a Spanish TV station...Javier plays on the ATP Tour and twice reached the quarterfinals of the U.S. Open...Arantxa authored a book titled "The Young Tennis Player: A Young Enthusiast's Guide to Tennis," which was published in 1996.

Career *Highlights*

Year	Achievement
1987	WTA Most Impressive Newcomer
1988	WTA Most Improved Player
1989	French Open Singles Champion
1990	French Open Mixed Doubles Champion
1991	Federation Cup Champion
1992	Australian Open Doubles Champion
1992	Olympic Bronze Medalist
1992	French Open Mixed Doubles Champion
1992	WTA Doubles Champion
1993	Federation Cup Champion
1993	U.S. Open Doubles Champion
1993	Australian Open Mixed Doubles Champion
1994	Federation Cup Champion
1994	French Open Singles Champion
1994	U.S. Open Singles & Doubles Champion
1994	ITF World Champion
1995	Federation Cup Champion
1995	Australian Open Doubles Champion
1995	Wimbledon Doubles Champion
1995	WTA Doubles Champion
1996	Olympic Silver Medalist
1996	Wins 500th Career Singles Match
1996	Australian Open Doubles Champion
1997	Tops $12 Million in Career Earnings
1998	French Open Singles Champion

who has been able to maintain her Top 10 ranking every season since—and that includes both Graf and Monica Seles! Every year brought Arantxa a new triumph. In 1990, she won the French Open mixed doubles title. In 1991, she led Spain to the Federation Cup. In 1992 and 1993 she won the Lipton Championship in Florida.

In 1994, 22-year-old Arantxa had her best season. She won eight singles championships, including the French Open and U.S. Open, and in seven of those tournaments she also took the doubles crown. Her U.S. championship was the first ever for a Spanish woman, and her $2.9 million in winnings was the most ever for a woman in any sport up to that time. At the end of the year, Arantxa was crowned WTA champion. She stayed hot right into the 1995 campaign, reaching the finals at the Australian Open and French Open and occupying the number-one spot in the world rankings for the first time in her career.

Although Arantxa is now considered one of the veterans of the women's tour, she has never lost the passion she brought to the sport when she was a wide-eyed teenager. And in many ways, she still takes the same childlike delight in tennis as she did when her dad first handed her that old Slazenger. "To me, tennis is a funny little ride," she says. "If you don't practice, and you don't want to play, you go down. But me, I run for all the balls and really enjoy playing. And no matter what, I always smile."

In 1990, Arantxa teamed with Martina Navratilova (left) to win her first career doubles championship. She has won over 50 more doubles titles since then.

ON HER MIND

"I try not to think about my opponent's game. I just go out on the court and play mine, to the best of my ability."

Monica Seles

T hank goodness for older brothers. Long before anyone had ever heard of Monica Seles, her brother Zoltan was one of the rising stars in Yugoslavian junior tennis. After six-year-old Monica watched the trophies and ribbons accumulate in his room, she started getting jealous. So she asked her father if he would teach her how to play. Karolj Seles was a cartoonist who had studied physical education in college, so he had an idea of how the body works. And what he did not know about tennis he read in books. He decided the most important thing he could teach Monica was to love the game. Then, if she showed any talent for tennis, he could find her a real coach.

Monica's dad drew pictures of Jerry, the cartoon mouse, on tennis balls and told Monica she was Tom, the cat. She would whack the ball with all her might. He also placed cute little stuffed animals on the ground and told Monica that she could keep the ones she hit with her shots. Sometimes, if Monica was doing something incorrectly, Karolj would draw a rabbit named "Little Mo" on a pad of paper, then flip the pages to make him move the way he wanted Monica to. This helped to teach her one of the most difficult tennis skills: hitting the ball on the rise. Monica's father also taught her to hit all of her groundstrokes with two hands, which was (and still is) considered very unusual.

Monica responds to her fans after winning her third straight Canadian Open. Her comeback ranks among the greatest ever.

Monica's two-handed forehand ranks among the most effective—and unusual—shots in the annals of tennis.

When Monica was six and a half, she entered her first tournament and reached the semifinals. By the age of nine she was the national 12-and-under champion for 1983. Monica won the European 12-and-unders in 1984 and 1985, and also won the '85 Orange Bowl 12-and-under title in Miami, Florida. There Monica met Nick Bollettieri, the famous tennis coach. He was impressed with her and gave her a full scholarship to his academy.

After adjusting to a new country, a new language and a new school, Monica flourished both on and off the court. By 1988, she was the best junior player anyone had ever seen. Bollettieri even thought she was good enough to beat some of the top pros. While still an amateur, Monica entered a couple of nearby tournaments and beat Helen Kelesi, and nearly defeated Chris Evert and Gabriela Sabatini. Based on these performances, she joined the WTA Tour in February of 1989.

Monica hit the pros like a hurricane. Her serve was accurate and had a deceptive spin, her baseline game was consistent and powerful, and she attacked any ball that was short and tried to put it away. Opponents were totally befuddled by her two-handed forehand—with the same motion, Monica could cream the ball down the sideline or snap a murderous cross-court shot. Also, Monica let out a loud and disconcerting "Eeeee-Uh!" whenever she hit a shot. "I've seen the tapes and I really can't believe it," she laughs. "It's unbelievable how hard I could hit the ball at that age."

Incredibly, Monica won the second tournament she entered as a pro, defeating Evert in the final. After her first year on the tour, Monica was ranked sixth in the world. In 1990, at the age of 16, she won three major events: the French Open, U.S. Hardcourts, and season-ending Virginia Slims Championships. She also edged Steffi Graf in the final of the German Open, beating the WTA's top-ranked player for the first time in her career. In 1991, Monica ended Graf's 186-week reign as the WTA's top player, and went on to take three Grand Slam titles, including the U.S. Open. In 1992, Monica became the first woman in more than half a century to win the French Open three years in a row, and she again won the Australian and U.S. titles. When she won the 1993 Australian Open, it marked her 30th singles championship in a span of less than three years. What she accomplished was simply amazing.

Monica's success was great for women's tennis at a time when the big names of the 1970s and 80s were slipping away. Her epic battles with Graf raised the level of both their games, and encouraged a new wave of teen stars to aim that much higher. Monica, in the meantime, was having a great time. She had grown into a confident, self-assured young woman who attacked life with the same gusto she attacked a tennis ball.

Getting Personal

Monica was born on December 2, 1973...She loved her first racket so much she slept with it every night...In Socialist Yugoslavia, tennis rackets were impossible to find. Karolj Seles had to drive 10 hours to Italy whenever Monica needed new equipment...Monica admitted "addiction" to butter cost her dearly during her two years of inactivity. At one point she ballooned to 160 pounds...During her rehab, she worked out with Olympic gold medalist Jackie Joyner-Kersee. "You would think that it would be intimidating to work out with Jackie," Monica says. "But she's the most down-to-earth person on earth."...Monica still stops to sign autographs for her fans after she is finished playing. "Some players only sign autographs when they win a match," she says. "I sign, win or lose."...Monica's father succumbed to cancer in the spring of 1998.

Career Highlights

Year	Achievement
1990	French Open Singles Champion
1990	WTA Most Improved Player
1991	Australian Open Singles Champion
1991	French Open Singles Champion
1991	U.S. Open Singles Champion
1991	WTA Player of the Year
1991	AP Female Athlete of the Year
1992	Australian Open Singles Champion
1992	French Open Singles Champion
1992	U.S. Open Singles Champion
1992	WTA Player of the Year
1992	AP Female Athlete of the Year
1993	Australian Open Slngles Champion
1995	WTA Comeback Player of the Year
1996	Australian Open Singles Champion
1996	Federation Cup Champion

Then, in one awful, unforgettable moment, Monica's world was shattered. During a match in Hamburg, Germany, a disturbed man named Gunther Parche worked his way to the railing and waited for Monica to sit down during a changeover. When she did, he pulled out a knife and attempted to plunge it into her back. Someone saw Parche and screamed, and luckily Monica lurched forward...just enough. The madman's knife only penetrated an inch into her body, near her left shoulder blade. The physical damage was relatively minor, but the emotional damage was severe.

After a few months, Monica's wound healed enough for her to start playing, but she was deeply depressed. She was outraged when Parche received a lenient sentence, and was shaken when she heard of the attack on skater Nancy Kerrigan. Monica began to wonder if any public figure was really safe. On top of this came the news that her father had cancer. Emotionally overwhelmed, she decided not to play tennis in 1994.

By the summer of 1995, however, Monica had whipped her demons and was back in fighting shape. Wishing to keep the media circus surrounding her comeback to a minimum, she chose for her return a medi-um-sized tournament, the Canadian Open. All she wanted was to last a couple of rounds and get the feel back. But to the complete astonishment of everyone—including Monica herself—she won! Then she nearly took the U.S. Open!

Monica continued her sensational comeback in 1996. She won the Australian Open and four other events, as well as reaching the final of the U.S. Open again. In 1997, she overcame a broken finger to win three tournaments (including the Canadian Open for the third year in a row), and reached the finals of the Lipton and Family Circle Cup.

Now in her mid-20s, Monica has to contend with a new group of hard-hitting teenage opponents, many of whom grew up idolizing *her*. And in what many view as a touching tribute, some of these young stars even let out little "Eeeee-Uh's" of their own.

Where Monica goes from here should be one of the most inter-esting stories in sports. She no longer plays for money and fame, but for the thrill of competition. She is also learning to love tennis again. Ironically, something that once came so naturally to Monica now requires as much hard work as any other part of her game.

Monica still hits with the same power that made her the game's number one player.

Venus & Serena
Williams

When people think about America's tennis "hotbeds," they picture the palm-lined courts of Florida, the sports-crazy suburbs of California, or some other upper middle-class enclave where tennis is practically a religion. In the Compton section of South Central Los Angeles, the religion is survival. Street gangs battle over turf, junkies and petty thieves steal anything that isn't nailed down, and mothers pray their children won't become the next victims of a stray bullet from a bad drug deal or drive-by shooting. "Gangs, drugs, crime—this place has it all," says Richard Williams. He should know. He managed to raise a couple of daughters in Compton. The amazing thing is that these young women—Venus and Serena—are considered the two best young tennis players in the United States.

Venus was four when her dad first took them to the local courts. A couple of years later, Serena, age five, joined them. Richard Williams knew they would be big, smart athletic girls, and believed tennis might open doors to a better life. Teaching from what he had read in tennis books and learned watching videos, Richard began to lay a foundation for his daughters. Because the courts separated rival gangs, he also had to teach them what to do when a gun battle erupted. It was not exactly the best place to learn tennis, but it was all they had. "The courts were always dirty and slippery," Venus remembers, "and the lights didn't come on, so we had to quit when it got too dark to see the balls."

As long as there was daylight, however, the Williams sisters made good use of it. They practiced endlessly, and even drew crowds of curious onlookers. Over the years, Venus and Serena became a source of tremendous pride for the people of Compton. They wanted them to make it out of the neighborhood and taste success in a world they would never know. Even the local gangs agreed not to fight around the tennis courts when the girls were playing.

Unlike their counterparts in high-priced teaching programs and academies, Venus and Serena lived normal lives when they walked off the

Venus (left) and her sister Serena have a bright future in front of them.

I like it when opponents fear me."

Serena hits a backhand to Irina Spirlea of Romania as she goes on to win her first round match at the 1998 Australian Open.

court each day. They went to school, made As and Bs, and played softball and kickball and ran races with their sisters, Isha, Lyndrea and Yelunde. But tennis was always the favorite. "I like the way it makes you think," Venus says. "And I like to blast the ball."

That was something both did extraordinarily well. Venus was quite tall for her age and could generate tremendous power, even at the age of 10. Some of her opponents could not even return her serves. If they did, she was usually stationed at the net, ready to bash a volley down their throats. Serena was not quite as tall, and had a little less natural ability, but that just made her work harder. Soon, she brought as much to the court as her older sister. When they played each other, they did so with the violence and passion of a street fight.

By 1991, Venus and Serena had advanced so rapidly that Richard knew they would need professional coaching. He moved the family to Delray Beach, Florida and enrolled his girls at a tennis school run by teaching pro Rick Macci. He did so with the understanding that they would *not* be playing in junior tournaments. Richard firmly believed that competing against children their own age would retard their progress. It was a controversial stance, and the tennis world reacted harshly. Coaches around the country believed that Richard had acted foolishly and that his inexperience in the sport would hurt his daughters. When asked why he kept his daughters out of the juniors, he would reply that he was only interested in the pros. When asked when he thought they would be ready, Richard said his daughters would let him know.

Richard Williams also came under fire for "auctioning off" Venus to the equipment company that offered the most money for her to endorse its products. He knew that many manufacturers thought the next growth area for U.S. tennis was likely to be the "ethnic" market. If so, he concluded, then Venus would be an incredibly valuable spokesperson for anyone trying to reach that market.

Getting Personal

Venus was born on June 17, 1980. Serena was born September 26, 1981...Venus has always had great speed and endurance. She ran a mile in 5:29 when she was only eight years old...Serena's approach to tennis is simple and direct: she wants to win every point...Venus likes to move in from the baseline and put the ball away. Opponents must concentrate on hitting deep shots or pay the consequences...Serena declined to play on the 1997 U.S. Federation Cup team because she wanted to devote full-time to her schoolwork. "I'm trying to get my diploma," she said. "My main goal this year is to get an A in Zoology. Fed Cup comes around the time I'm taking my final exams."...The two sisters faced each other as pros for the first time in the second round of the 1998 Australian Open. Venus won 7-6, 6-1. "I'm sorry to take you out," she said to Serena. "I didn't want to, but I had to. Let's make sure next time it's in a final so it will be for a title."...Both sisters wear beads in their hair when they play, Venus prefers blue and white and Serena prefers yellow.

Eventually, he got millions for Venus and lined up lucrative deals for Serena, too. A lot of tennis traditionalists thought it vulgar to take advantage of this situation, especially with a girl so young. But as others were quick to point out, it was the traditionalists who had long excluded African-Americans, Asian-Americans and Hispanics from the sport—and that was even *more* distasteful.

Career *Highlights*

Year	Venus' Achievements
1997	US Open Singles FInalist
1997	WTA Most Impressive Newcomer
1998	Lipton Singles Champion
1998	French Open Mixed Doubles Champion

Year	Serena's Achievements
1997	Beat Top-10 Players in 13th & 14th Career Matches
1998	Lipton Singles Quarterfinalist

Over the next few years, Venus and Serena played against each other and the pros at Macci's, and worked hard to improve in all areas. It was not unusual for them to practice six hours a day, and they regularly squeezed off 200 serves in an afternoon. Finally, the big day came. In the fall of 1994, Venus played and won her first pro match against Shaun Stafford at a tournament in Oakland, California. In the second round, 14-year-old Venus—who now stood six feet tall—took the first set from Arantxa Sanchez Vicario, the world's number two player. Sanchez Vicario managed to recover and squeak out a victory, but Venus had made a huge impression. It was a couple of more years, however, before Venus was allowed to play a full schedule. Mostly, she stayed home in Florida and hit with pros. Serena, meanwhile, was developing an awesome power game. All that remained for her was to bring it under control.

The 1997 season saw Venus make her big breakthrough. She played well all summer, and shot up the rankings. At the U.S. Open, Venus got hot and made it all the way to the finals, where she fell to Martina Hingis. In 1998, Venus continued to improve. After reaching the finals at the Adidas International in Sydney, Australia, and the quarterfinals of the Australian Open, she won her first career event, the IGA Tennis Classic in Oklahoma City. She then defeated Hingis and Anna Kournikova to win the prestigious Lipton Cup.

Meanwhile, Serena was making a name for herself. Though she declared herself a professional in 1995, she did not hit the pro tour for real until 1997. At the Ameritech Cup in Chicago, she reached the semis in singles by beating Mary Pierce and Monica Seles. Never before in the history of the WTA Tour had a player ranked so low (453 at the time) beaten two Top 10 opponents in the same event. That put Serena in the Top 100 after just six tournaments. In 1998, she reached the semifinals at Sydney, the quarterfinals in Oklahoma, and nearly beat Hingis in the quarters at the Lipton. Heading into the heart of her first Grand Slam season, Serena was on the verge of cracking the Top 20. More important, she was no longer "Venus's little sister."

How far Venus and Serena Williams go on the pro tour is anyone's guess. Given their considerable skills and remarkable progress, there is every reason to believe they will be squaring off for a major championship in the not-too-distant future. More intriguing, however, is where they will take the sport itself. For decades, tennis people have wondered what would happen if the game could "reach into" the inner cities and pluck out the cream of the athletic crop. It looks as if they're about to get their answer.

Venus is one of the most physically gifted players in the history of women's tennis. Her serve may one day be the best in the game.

"I'm tall. I'm black. Everything's different about me. Just face the facts."

What's Next

O ne of the truly nice things about tennis is that it has never been about being the biggest or the fastest or the strongest. It has always been about being the *best*. If you look at all the number one players over the past century, the most striking thing you find is that, physically, they were no more impressive than the dozen-or-so players nipping at their heels. What set them apart was the huge emotional and intellectual investment they made in the game. They gave fully of themselves to tennis, committing their bodies and souls to the sport.

The great champions were not born this way. They came to it through endless hours of practice, years of competition, and more mistakes and humiliation than any of them care to remember.

Nowadays, women are reaching the threshold of greatness in tennis before they are allowed to sip their first beer. Has the game changed so much? Are the athletes that much better? The answer to both questions is *yes*...and *no*.

Tennis is basically the same game it has always been. Like all sports, it has evolved, but it is not radically different than it was, say, five or 10 years ago. Where women's tennis has changed dramatically in a relatively short amount of time is in training techniques, sports medicine, nutrition, and the emotional path players travel to the pros. This combination—and in particular that last item—has an awful lot to do with what is happening in tennis today.

Gifted players are culled much sooner and handled much more differently than in the past. Whereas, during the 1970s and 80s, a promising 11-year-old might have been hardened in junior competition for a pro career beginning at age 18, today's ingenue is expected to be "tour-ready" by the time she is 16. She will spend less time slogging through tournaments and more time working with top coaches, who will hone every aspect of her game, from her groundstrokes to her mental approach. By the time she hits the WTA Tour, she is a voracious winner who only knows one way to deal with an opponent: nuke her.

So does that make her a better athlete? Not necessarily. To get a little kid ready for the big time, some important corners get cut. Although the teenagers on the pro tour today are bigger and faster and stronger than ever, they are ill-equipped to deal with the grind of playing tennis for a living. They also don't know how to learn from their losses. When all you have experienced in your young life is winning, it is hard to find anything positive about losing match after match to older, more experienced opponents.

As for the players who do manage to rise to the top of the rankings, yes, they *are* better athletes than their predecessors. Having overcome the psychological barriers of tennis, they are free to let their physical genius flow. And sometimes being a little bigger, a little faster or a little stronger does have its advantages.

Is tennis about to be overrun by heavily-muscled six-footers with Olympic-sprinter speed? No, that won't happen. And that is because tennis remains the game it always has been. Drive and desire will always win out over a 100-mile-per-hour serve, and a sharp mind will eventually find a way to undo a booming backhand. That is not to say, however, that a "super player" won't be coming along one of these days. She might even be playing right this very minute. But if that does happen—if someone bursts onto the scene and simply overwhelms the competition—that will only make the women's game stronger. Indeed, if history teaches us one thing, it is that the rest of the players will only get better. And they *will* find a way to bring her down.

INDEX

PAGE NUMBERS IN ITALICS REFER TO ILLUSTRATIONS.

9482